**Feed**

# Sunken Garden Poetry at Hill-Stead Museum

Sunken Garden Poetry began in 1992 in Farmington, Connecticut, with a single poetry reading in the magical setting of Hill-Stead Museum's Sunken Garden, drawing a huge crowd even that first year. Since then the annual series has become one of the premiere and best-loved venues for poetry in the country, featuring the top tier of American poets as well as emerging and student writers from the region. From its inception twenty years ago, this poetry festival has given equal weight to the quality of text and the poet's ability to deliver an engaging, powerful, and entertaining experience in the unique theater of the Sunken Garden.

Out of the festival have grown competitions, year-round workshops and events, and an educational outreach to Hartford high schools. And while centered at Hill-Stead—with its beautiful views, Colonial Revival house, and priceless collection of Impressionist paintings—Sunken Garden Poetry now engages an ever wider audience through a growing online presence; an online poetry journal, *Theodate* (http://theodate.org); public radio broadcasts; and an annual chapbook prize, now co-published by Tupelo Press.

## Sunken Garden Poetry Prize

2014
*We Practice for It,* by Ted Lardner. Selected by Mark Doty

2015
*Fountain and Furnace,* by Hadara Bar-Nadav. Selected by Peter Stitt

2016
*Feed,* by Suzanne Parker. Selected by Jeffrey Levine and Cassandra Cleghorn

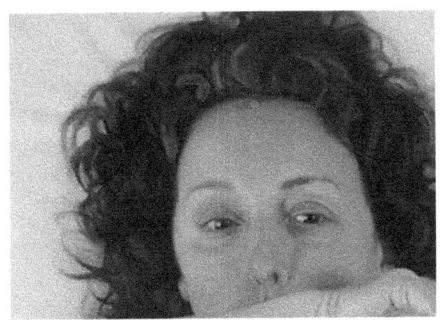

# FEED
Suzanne Parker

Tupelo Press
North Adams, Massachusetts

*Feed.*
Copyright © 2016 Suzanne Parker. All rights reserved.

ISBN 978-1-936797-87-5

Cover and text designed by Bill Kuch.
Cover: Lee Price, "Jelly Doughnuts." Oil on linen (40" x 64").
Copyright © 2010 Lee Price (www.leepricestudio.com). Used with permission of the artist.

First paperback edition: June 2016.

Other than brief excerpts for reviews and commentaries, no part of this book may be reproduced by any means without permission of the publisher. Please address requests for reprint permission or for course-adoption discounts to:

Tupelo Press
P.O. Box 1767, 243 Union Street, Eclipse Mill, Loft 305
North Adams, Massachusetts 01247
Telephone: (413) 664–9611 / editor@tupelopress.org
www.tupelopress.org

Tupelo Press is an award-winning independent literary press that publishes fine fiction, nonfiction, and poetry in books that are a joy to hold as well as read. Tupelo Press is a registered 501(c)(3) nonprofit organization, and we rely on public support to carry out our mission of publishing extraordinary work that may be outside the realm of large commercial publishers. Financial donations are welcome and are tax deductible.

*For my parents, who filled the house with art and music.*

## Contents

- *3* • Feed
- *4* • Possibly Picasso's
- *5* • This
- *7* • The Cut-Out Operation
- *15* • Mulberry Picking
- *16* • White Underside of Turkey Feather against Green Slope
- *17* • Gauguin in Paradise
- *18* • It Is Raining inside My Skin
- *20* • Like the gulls
- *22* • So I buy a record of Fernanda Maria because
- *23* • Breaking Down
- *25* • As in the Poem
- *26* • Woman at the Center of the Gaze
- *27* • After Miró
- *28* • Rule Book
- *29* • Metrics
- *30* • Small Oranges on a Platter
- *31* • Thirst
- *32* • The Just-Cut Field
- *33* • TheVeryMany
- *34* • The Museum-Goer's Strategy

- *37* • Notes
- *38* • Acknowledgments

**Feed**

## Feed

The red fox keeps killing
the neighbor's chickens
for the thrill of it,
for bone-snap and heat
and stain and greed and warm
blood flooding the mouth,
for snarl and legs and the cornered
shiver of white feathers
in a viscous breeze,
for the low belly, tail high,
that declaration aflame
in the field and fast, fast
before it's even dragged
the last meat off the bone
it is looking at the few hens
scratching in the rafters, as if
heat could be cloaked
by dark, as if their cries
weren't already his,
as if desire could be salved
with one small meal.

## Possibly Picasso's

lady has dropped her own eyeball into her lap on purpose
so the other can circle the fishbowl of her thoughts.

Perhaps she wished to turn blind toward the future,
surprise snickering the smooth lake of her days.

Or, something shattered, split, the bedrock
of her bones shifting, and like cars, streets,

whole buildings bursting with living, it dropped
into what no longer was, though maybe

as the catalog says of this fractured green
and orange woman whose lips have slipped

onto her arm like a band of brazen mourning:
*What is to be carefully noticed,* it goes on,

*She has not yet* though *Note the scarlet cast*
but maybe *Her watching is self-determination,*

*but in the outlines.* In another second *You
will see,* she will pull herself together into

what she is: cantaloupe slices on a platter,
coveted by a cloud of fruit flies.

**This**

begins where the city's streets
string white lights across their throats

when most have shut their doors,
reduced the living to one room.

This turns with the underside
of the waiter's wrist clearing dishes,

a small table cluttered with utensils
dangerously nestled together,

and I have eased off my heels
beneath the table, the last customer,

the last sip of red, this like
words translated from the menu—

*trout in heavy sweater* and *flavored
fir tree buds,* even *softened*

*eggs of the large birds*— and ladle
after ladle of fire over custard,

*the burning pudding,* and I unhook
the spoon from its mate, fill its belly

with the first, best bite, ferry it
across this night, this city, the river

swallowing its stories in a hush,
just outside. This won't stop: *salad*

*of goat heat,* flow and flight, consuming
this language in its *silk dress of cream.*

## The Cut-Out Operation

*after Matisse*

i.

I dream my room is an egg,
the yolk sucked out
from a small hole in the ceiling.
I curve into the white surrounds,
watch a silent, un-shifting blue.


ii.

Room after room after room;
generations linked like train cars
attached in different countries,
the only continuity— intention.


iii.

Matisse used black
to paint light
so the white curtains,
swelling like a shroud
stuffed with anemones,
the sweat of salt,
discarded carmine
of emptied crab shells,

are barred at the top in black
as if to say— *Go. Yes, go.*


iv.

The floor is bleached
with sun. I realize
that blue is a window
and the red goldfish
are not swimming
through a storm.
No. It is a shower
of white light.


v.

The sea intrudes on the room.
Boats perch like gulls
on the balcony railing.
Someone has painted the calm
from this day—
those brutal boys—
and, once again,
thick black outlines
like punctuation.


vi.
In all that he has flattened—
view, Seine, chair and

his own self on it,
eye like a collapsed box
on the floor— the tall green
arch of a plant sways,
dips its neck to taste
the water in the bowl beneath
and this is how it will begin.


vii.

Extreme emphatic frontality—
the wide black mullion
down the center and like a pin
piercing a tie the glass bowl,
its provocation of red,
fish so quickly painted
they could be a slip
of the tongue.


viii.

Such angularity:
the jackknife of knee,
thigh, calf, crease
of pant-edge outlined
like a strike against
a broken silence.

ix.

After you finish reading,
I can see your skin,
the way sunlight pierces
what is sheer, turns it
into its own ghost.


x.

I am a book, spine
against palm; you halt
the inevitable fall
and spillage, letters chattering
against the walls.


xi.

When the day is reduced
to hyphens/dashes
and my breath like shattered glass
across the floor,
you turn from me—
and I curl myself
like a small hermit inside her shell.

xii.

And the thumb
pressing through
the palette's
opening,
wandering the air—
soft medallion.


xiii.

There is a certain kind of blue:
cerulean. You against
a swath of sea and fence
of wind. Your jacket
across my back.

Blue like herons
and their harpoons aimed,
wings like something opened
then broken.


xiv.

If you did look,
what is there?
Angle, the flat
blue lick
that was river

and all its people
strolling, kissing,
posing for the picture,
now gone, lightened
of their stories.
If you look
out my window,
is there a view
or the lines
that speak of shutters?

xv.

Between heat
and touch,
a late afternoon
turns on itself.
In a tabletop bowl
of luminosity,

wet your fingers.
Let the fish nibble.
In this painting,
the hour does not end.

xvi.

I dream in French
words I've never spoken—

silks, *les soies,* pulled
from my mouth.
You bind my wrists.
*Quel est le mot?*
This liminal phase—
*arche, intention, la langue.*
*Un après-midi pris derrière les volets.*


xvii.

One could argue perspective—
flat and color blocks—
but there is also the swell
of flock, mid-air,
its change of mind,
how that withdrawal aches,
must empty the wind
of its intention, all this
begs for curve, sway,
heat, the weight of one
body descending upon another.


xviii.

His world outside—
how simple
to muffle it.  In less time
than it took to open
the window; a few quick

brush strokes and—
past the railing,
where there
had been view— now,
simply, blue.
This new kind of blue.

## Mulberry Picking

I don't think the orioles know their own splendor.

I don't think the mulberry tree knows it shivers as it holds them.

I don't think the berries' juice can slake any thirst as large as this

yet I march out each morning, colander in hand and beneath

the outrage of the crows pick what is difficult, sweet, what stains

under the nails and seeps into the tracks we all carry in our skin;

like a river, my greed flows purple, fast, and thunders

throughout the day, marking me for all to see.

## White Underside of Turkey Feather against Green Slope

Sweat like paste and the scent
of vanilla.  Summer
at a highway rest stop—

the sluggish heat and heart
of oil, gas, the stalled adventure.
So one fear pulls in all the others

and the tires swoosh to the rhythm of
want, want, want.  It breathes
against the cars' windows

and a girl in the back seat
emblazons her initials.  I see them
carved against her cheek

as they ramp up to speed, so I steal this,
the only thing with grace;
everything else is exhaust and sky.

## Gauguin in Paradise

The card reads: *As suggested by the thick
black line.* Indeed, the women swell

against their limits, this *his
full bloom primitivistic Tahitian period,*

a man says before a platter of fruit
and breasts. Your note says: *Cream*

*we have. If you'll get coffee.* I know
there is charcoal sketching my skin.

I smudge what I touch, think color
has its own mind. I cannot get it right.

I came to you with bags full
of small desires but standing

before the Gauguins, I see
a woman swallowing her own arm,

think this is how to change
the shape, know this woman

caught in his remembering.
It states: *Some areas were left bare—*

*naked canvas.* My eye
smearing what surrounds.

## It Is Raining inside My Skin

*Heard during an NPR interview*

Perhaps schizophrenia gives her
a new vocabulary of sense, perhaps

it has many words for sad and touch
and truth and how the body

can be the world like the butter
the croissant exhales and I suck

deep inside my lungs to lock there
or the ease with which you smooth

me into sleep, and on the banks of the Seine
that time, thick crowds ate, shifted,

ignored the spectacle of setting sun,
which some might call flame burning

the ladder of the spine, and the stamp
of Notre Dame against the sky, the spread

legs of the river, two islands nestled
between her knees, one tucked

behind the other.  Everything is erotic.
You pass me the bread and cheese.

I give you the night, filling
the bottom of a pilfered glass

which some might call thievery but maybe
is just another form of swallowing.

## Like the gulls

that stalk the beach,
appetite is about fear—

not enough, no seconds, none
for you, the small orphan Oliver's

hollow bowl and his stomach
like our selves, caves that swallow

and are empty again
and always, so always this.

It is not hunger that starts the jets
of saliva, that orders from both sides

of the menu then calls the waiter back,
asks of sides: potatoes in cream,

the fallen stalks of asparagus, roasted garlic
in cheese with lime.  No.  Hunger

listens to be called inside
where it slides into place at the table,

smooths a napkin across the lap.
But, appetite is not called.  It sneaks,

sidles, swoons at the trays of pastries
in the window, weeps as it slips the first

bite between the lips.  This is what fear
tastes of: butter, honey, and glass.

## So I buy a record of Fernanda Maria because

she raises her thick eyebrows like Frida Kahlo
because an ink black shawl slashes across her breasts,
and she juts out her chin,
looks down her nose
because you have left me,
and she seems like she could handle it.

So I buy the record with sing-a-long text
because *Fadista!* is a word I'd like
to own as an antidote to others—
poetess, niceness, possess, these leaking
mouthfuls, how they lack the bullet
puncturing the earth at its end. I imagine hips.

Because as the text says: *Life is short;*
*we cannot prevent its sorrows.* Because
*Fado and the bulls are the great pleasures,*
and my father studied the corrida; he too is gone.
Everything now is *saudade,* the nostalgia

of the empty arena. The air has replaced you
beside me. So I will take Fernanda Maria
from her covers and let the needle wake her
to rough consonants and exclamation points,
the guttering of vowels in an empty throat.

## Breaking Down

the folds into categories.
The book says this is about
tone: *a test of finesse.*

In the tumult of sheets,
the peaks and valleys
of remembering, *consider*

*depth.* Hold the pencil
as if about to drop it,
as if a snake. *Heavy fingers,*

*a tight grip are the sign*
*of inexperience.* There is
too much sway and cave

in my still life. Too much
murk beneath the bright.
*Removed from bodies,*

*drawing shadows can seem*
*without purpose* but heat
lingers. How do I

sketch the crease left
in the pillow? The shower
is already on. *You need*

*to know the characteristics
of types.* The three
kinds of lead. *Do not fear

blending. Use your index
finger to rub away the edges.*
It says I can erase. It says,

the book, there is much more
practice necessary. *In the eye
pleasure and in the thumbs.*

## As in the Poem

*Sticks stubble the breeze*
and *There are certain nests lined with our names.*

If she says, *My fingers identify your fear.*
*Snuff it out. Wear the smudge on my forehead until dusk.*

As in, *Too many poems about mothers and their milk*
for *She never picked me up and you.*

If, *I offer you my soul's thin jacket and its shoes*
but *The park digs its own moat and we without our fish feet.*

Then, *If you travel the continent of my back*
*with the boat of your hand.* In sum,

*Kiss me* the poem does not say, but the vowels
turn on their bellies *In the silence of your going.*

## Woman at the Center of the Gaze

*To facilitate the formation of a mental image, we may repeat our sensation by studying a model.* —Paul Sérusier

He said take your bra off and she
unwrapped herself from one, two,
three, her skin glowing brighter
and him feeling his chest tighten.

He asked how many were left her
and she raised her eyes— she did
truly love him— and opened her mouth
to say she did not know but instead

silk unfurled down the runway
of her thoughts and he caught
the sailing flag and pulled,
threads unraveling around him,

slipping beneath his arms, lifting
his chin until he too was flying.

## After Miró

*Why is your mouth here?*

You will need those

        two dropped thoughts

                reddening

on your belly. Let me take my hands,

        their ten winged fingers, scoop

                what is lost

into the green air. Let me

        take my eyes and like guests

                enter the just opened doors.

In the safety of his thick black lines,

        we are circling,

                lip and    lip and    lip and    lip.

## **Rule Book**

If I eat your face, I am insane.
If I nibble your lip, I am in love.
Such distinctions to keep in mind.

If I give you my right hand, I want you
to lay me across the bed of the day,
sing songs into wherever I open.  If

I offer you my left, I plan on sipping tea
with the rest of the world while you drink
alone the Bitter Bitches from the fridge.

If I walk past our building, look up and see you,
the rules of distance will collapse.
If I note the rough tongue of pavement,

bicycles will roll un-ridered down city streets
into the chaos of traffic, the decisions
of stop or go, turn or straight, hope or cry.

If your voice swirls in the cups of my ears,
I will collect its letters, stash them in a box
behind my ribs.  If you come to claim them,

we can spread them on the table, build towers,
knock them down.  We can make
our own game's rules, then cheat.

## Metrics

What is the word for air
hitting the throat's back?

How do I spell a question
living inside the jar

of my days?  What is
the syntax of knees

held open, the bridge
of hips?  When you kiss

the language from my hours,
some fierce animal in me

circles twice around herself
and settles at the bottom

of a vowel.  How does caught
breath scan?  Your pulse or mine?

## **Small Oranges on a Platter**

You do not need to say desire—
laid out in daylight
on a sideboard
as if there
they will be harmless
as if peel stripped
won't leave a scent
beneath the nails as if,
later, you will not
raise your fingers,
think of separating
the body, section
by section.  Use
the word swallow.
Notice the lips' position—
without restraint,
in the middle,
how they open.

## Thirst

The rain is consumed by the sea, its dark, unquenchable thirst. *I need,*
the girl whines, hanging off her mother's hand, knowing her thirst.

The salt of the waves prickles the air, is lifted from the skin. Later
after swallowing oceans, we stumble to the fridge and slake our thirst.

Every morning demands its ransom, and we untangle legs from legs.
Every story has an other moving to the well, bucket swinging with thirst.

Summer soon. The world will shake her thermometer and sweat. Once,
we thought the ices singeing our throats were all there ever was of thirst.

You ask me to dance on the lip of the night and I gather up my skirt.
Bring me champagne, gallons, a sea, your mouth. I have such a thirst.

## The Just-Cut Field

The dog keeps eating shit
and dead things— mice, snakes,
dismembered frogs— but, first,
he rolls in them. A shoulder,
the belly, then a quick flip
and the whole of him shifting
left and right, rubbing himself against
what the just-cut hay and blades
have revealed. There is no
calling him off his delirium,
tongue agog, hunting, refusing
to loop the field as we usually do,
but smashing forward to find
what only his nose knows
as pleasure. He leaves me stranded
between the choices—
watch and wait as he zigzags
to the logic of desire
or pull him back, clip on the leash.

## TheVeryMany

She is a fury of concentration,
small body boomeranging

against the sharp edges
of possibility. No entry.

Letters capped, in bold.
A museum guard is rigid

beside the mammoth metal shell
punched with stars, a jitterbug

of light and space the girl knows
as she does settling between

the willow's roots, her name
shifting the branches as her mother

calls from the door yet again.
Something about crawling inside.

The girl licks the stale air as she tilts
and slants her gaze higher, noting

foot and handholds. All that smooth,
cool steel. If not in, then up.

## The Museum-Goer's Strategy

Don't start with the Madonna
dead on the table.
*Go back.*
Start with the hours walking
the cool-draped halls, looking
for the open window
to show the rain has stopped
and it is time to go out
away from the grand relay of art—
triptych to French fowl,
head limp on a platter with
a lemon and glass of white wine.

*Start earlier*

The flight to Paris, plane's
ascension, nails half moons
in Lori's hand, and before us,
always before us, the idea
packed in a suitcase,
embarrassed to be seen with—
Hemingway, Stein, Fischer
snuck in as contraband—

*and before this*

the Hoshi on the wall
of my mother's living room:
a single tree, limned
in gold, painted blue and alone
against a flat horizon or

*even farther*

my father's bonsais, those islands,
each with its own palm-tree
and castaway sunk in the still study,
and no one could keep
them alive after his death.

*Start sooner*

with the shock
he spent a summer bullfighting,
learning to plant his feet, practicing
the verónicas, cape crimsoning the air,

*No. Sooner*

like the opera always playing
in the background of memories,
the control required as the scale
is strung, the huge leap
to find the upper notes, stay
in one place, paint a solitary tree.

*I have flown*

six hours to be where I am,
finally, stopped before
Caravaggio's rejected Mary,
the one too gray, too swollen,
too naked. The museum asks
in five languages for its patrons
to leave. Now, it is time to start.

Notes

"The Cut-Out Operation" is a response to the Art Institute of Chicago's 2010 exhibit, "Matisse: Radical Invention, 1913–1917."

The epigraph for "Woman at the Center of the Gaze" is from "The ABC of Painting" by Paul Sérusier, which appeared in *Art and Literature: An International Quarterly* (Issue 11, Winter 1967).

"TheVeryMany" is the name of a sculpture by Marc Fornes at the Centre Georges Pompidou in Paris.

## Acknowledgments

I am grateful to the Vermont Studio Center for time to work on these poems. Thanks also to the editors of the following journals in which versions of these poems have appeared or are forthcoming.

*B O D Y:* "Rule Book"
*The Boiler:* "The Just-Cut Field" and "Thirst"
*Clockhouse:* "Gauguin in Paradise"
*Diode:* "As in the Poem," "Like the gulls," and "Metrics"
*Interim:* "TheVeryMany"
*The Literary Bohemian:* "The Museum-Goer's Strategy"
*Notre Dame Review:* "It Is Raining inside My Skin"
*Passages North:* "Possibly Picasso's" and "This"
*Redivider:* "Small Oranges on a Platter"
*Tampa Review:* "So I buy a record of Fernanda Maria"
*The 2River View:* "Feed" and "Mulberry Picking"

## Other Books from Tupelo Press

*Fasting for Ramadan* (memoir), Kazim Ali
*Pulp Sonnets* (poems, with drawings by Amin Mansour), Tony Barnstone
*Brownwood* (poems), Lawrence Bridges
*Everything Broken Up Dances* (poems), James Byrne
*One Hundred Hungers* (poems), Lauren Camp
*New Cathay: Contemporary Chinese Poetry* (anthology), edited by Ming Di
*Entwined: Three Lyric Sequences* (poems), Carol Frost
*Poverty Creek Journal* (lyric memoir), Thomas Gardner
*The Good Dark* (poems), Annie Guthrie
*The Faulkes Chronicle* (novel), David Huddle
*Halve* (poems), Kristina Jipson
*Darktown Follies* (poems), Amaud Jamaul Johnson
*Dancing in Odessa* (poems), Ilya Kaminsky
*Third Voice* (poems), Ruth Ellen Kocher
*Boat* (poems), Christopher Merrill
*A Camouflage of Specimens and Garments* (poems), Jennifer Militello
*Lucky Fish* (poems), Aimee Nezhukumatathil
*The Ladder* (poems), Alan Michael Parker
*Weston's Unsent Letters to Modotti* (poems), Chad Parmenter
*Ex-Voto* (poems), Adélia Prado, translated by Ellen Doré Watson
*Mistaking Each Other for Ghosts* (poems), Lawrence Raab
*Intimate: An American Family Photo Album* (hybrid memoir), Paisley Rekdal
*Thrill-Bent* (novel), Jan Richman
*Swallowing the Sea* (essays), Lee Upton
*Butch Geography* (poems), Stacey Waite

See our complete list at www.tupelopress.org

www.ingramcontent.com/pod-product-compliance
Lightning Source LLC
Chambersburg PA
CBHW040312050426
42450CB00020B/3466